BOOK HOUSE
Life-Sized
Animal
POO

AUTHOR:
John Townsend

WILDLIFE CONSULTANT:
The National Poo Museum

Contents

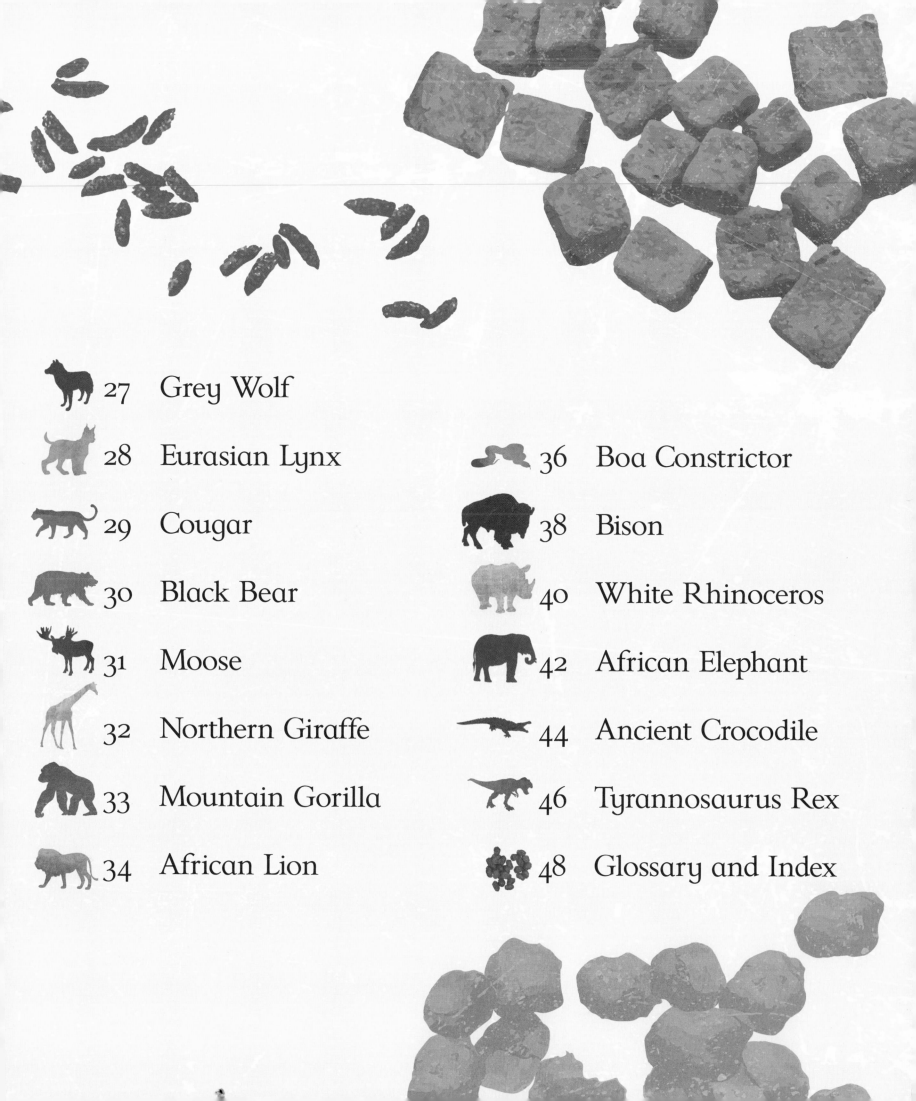

Introduction

Animal poo can tell us a lot about the wild animal that left it behind. The shape, size, colour and texture of animal poo help experts know which animals are in an area and exactly where different species are living. Scientists also study droppings to find out how healthy an animal is, what it has eaten and important information about a habitat.

You might be surprised by some of the secrets hidden in different types of animal poo. Inside these pages you are about to get to the bottom of a fascinating subject!

Some animals leave sausage-shaped poo, some drop lumps, pellets or splats, and others poop hairy twists or curls. Whatever the type, all animal poo is called 'scat' by trackers.

Any animal's poo size will vary from day to day, so the samples here show an average.

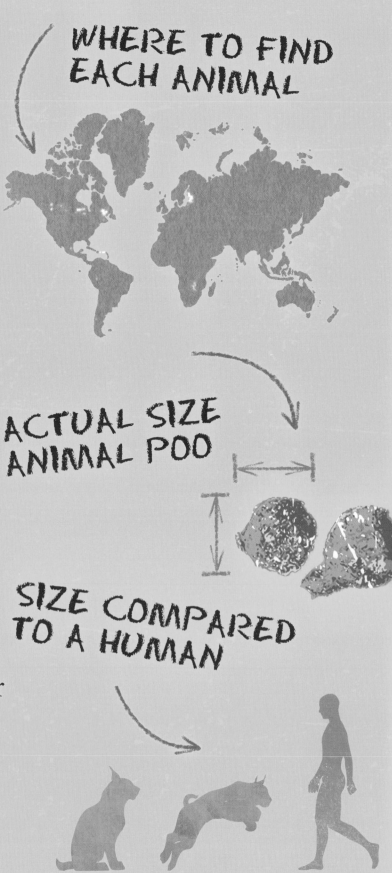

WHERE TO FIND EACH ANIMAL

ACTUAL SIZE ANIMAL POO

SIZE COMPARED TO A HUMAN

Brown Long-eared Bat

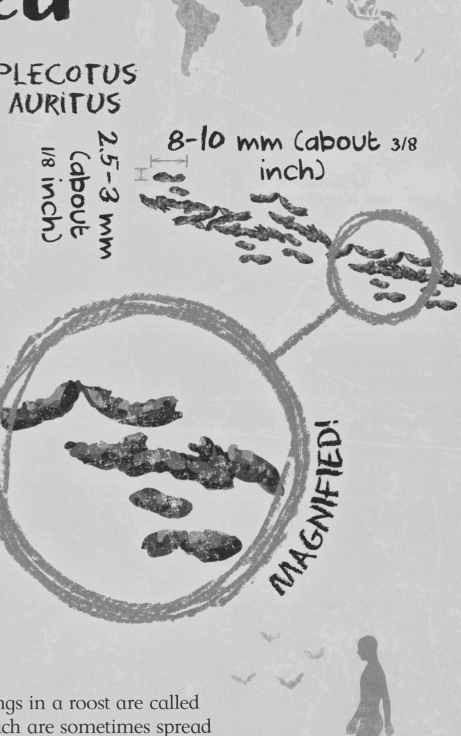

PLECOTUS AURITUS

2.5–3 mm (about 1/8 inch)

8–10 mm (about 3/8 inch)

MAGNIFIED!

There are many species of bat around the world and brown long-eared bats are easy to identify because their ears are almost as long as their bodies. They fly from their roosts after sunset to catch flying insects. They often eat their prey while hanging upside down, leaving piles of insect remains on the ground below. When it's time to poo, they just flip over so they don't poo over themselves.

The bats' droppings are dark knobbly grains only a few millimetres long. When crumbled between the fingers and held up to the light, these sparkle with the shimmering insect wings inside them.

Bat droppings in a roost are called guano, which are sometimes spread on soil to make rich fertilizer. Caves where bats have lived over hundreds of years can have layers of guano up to 20 metres (66 feet) deep.

House Mouse

MUS MUSCULUS

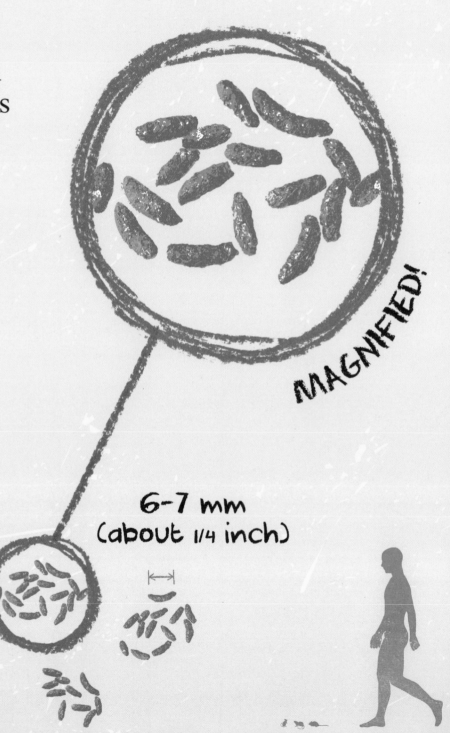

The common house mouse is a major rodent pest in most parts of the world. A female can give birth to 12 babies every three weeks, which could mean 150 offspring in a year.

House mice eat most things, which is why they are pests when they come indoors and nibble everything. Even a small group of mice can leave thousands of tiny droppings in a short time. An adult house mouse usually leaves 70 to over 100 droppings per day - dark pellets pointed at each end.

Fresh droppings are a deep, shiny black. Older droppings tend to be faded and will crumble easily. Mice often eat their own droppings to get nutrients from the bacteria inside.

MAGNIFIED!

6-7 mm (about 1/4 inch)

Brown Rat

RATTUS NORVEGICUS

The brown rat has many names, including common rat, street rat, sewer rat, Hanover rat and Norway rat. Its body grows up to 30 cm (11.8 inches), with its tail almost as long.

Like all rodents, brown rats have sharp front teeth that constantly grow. They chew on wood to keep the teeth short and sharp. Just like mice, rats eat almost anything and leave behind plenty of dark droppings.

20 mm (about 3/4 inch)

4 mm (about 1/8 inch)

MAGNIFIED!

Brown rat droppings are larger than those of mice and are more oval-shaped, like olive stones. They are usually scattered in a mass rather than as single pellets.

Eastern Chipmunk
TAMIAS STRIATUS

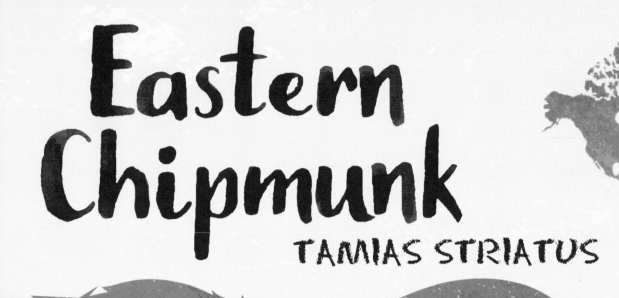

O ver 20 different species of chipmunk live in North America. One of the smaller species is the Eastern chipmunk, which grows to about 30 cm (11.8 inches) long, including its bushy tail.

Chipmunks are often seen as pests because they eat most things, including bulbs, seeds, fruits, nuts, plants, insects, worms and even birds' eggs. The Eastern chipmunk crams food into its cheek pouches as a takeaway to eat later.

8–10 mm
(about 3/8 inch)

Chipmunk droppings are like dark grains of rice. They're similar to mouse droppings, but slightly larger and harder.

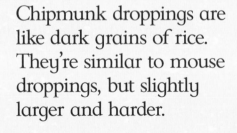

Grey Squirrel

SCIURUS CAROLINENSIS

4 mm (about 1/8 inch)

10 mm (about 3/8 inch)

The North American grey squirrel was brought to the UK in the 1800s and is now common in British woodlands, parks and gardens. Grey squirrels make a rough nest, called a drey, out of twigs, leaves and strips of bark in trees. Females may have two litters of three to four young a year.

Squirrels eat tree bark, buds, berries, seeds, acorns and nuts, which they often bury in the ground to store for the winter.

Grey squirrel droppings are pellets that are rounded at the ends, unlike the more pointed poo left by rats. The colour lightens over time.

Raven
CORVUS CORAX

Ravens are relatives of crows and look similar. Both are black birds with large, heavy bills. A crow's tail is shaped like a fan, while the raven's tail is wedge-shaped.

Ravens are intelligent birds that can often work out how to get food from places difficult to reach, such as inside rubbish bins.

25–30 mm (about 1 inch)

Raven droppings can be difficult to identify as they are usually white, runny and dropped from a great height. When pooed directly on the ground, the droppings don't tend to splat and are easier to study.

Scientists have even studied raven poo to find out which birds are the most stressed!

Pheasant
PHASIANUS COLCHICUS

Pheasants are related to wild chickens and live in woods, fields, grassland and scrub where they stay on the ground most of the time. They are often raised as game birds to be hunted and eaten. They can fly at speeds of up to 72 kph (45 mph) for short distances.

Pheasants eat seeds, berries, grain, fruit, insects and small reptiles. They can survive in cold climates by digging through snow to find food in winter.

20 mm
(about 3/4 inch)

Pheasant droppings look like 2 cm (0.8 inch) long sausages. They look like soft ice cream; grey-green, coated in white liquid waste called uric acid.

MAGNIFIED!

Green Woodpecker
PICUS VIRIDIS

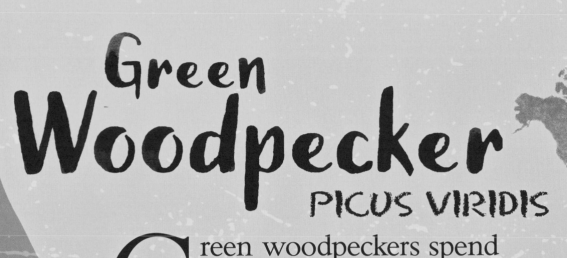

Green woodpeckers spend most of their time feeding on the ground or pecking at tree trunks. Male and female green woodpeckers look similar, but adult males have more red around their beak, like a moustache.

30–50 mm (about 1 1/2 inches)

For most of the year, green woodpeckers live alone until they nest in holes which they peck in dead wood. They have a distinct call which is like a loud laugh, known as a 'yaffle'.

Green woodpeckers eat insects - especially ants, which they dig out from ant nests with their strong beaks. Their droppings are usually full of ant remains. Their sausage-shaped poo contains a splash of white uric acid.

Canada Goose
BRANTA CANADENSIS

Canada geese are easily recognised by their black head and neck, white cheeks and chin, and brown body. They are native to North America but they migrate to northern Europe, including the UK. They can often be found on or close to fresh water, where they like to graze on grasses. Canada geese will also eat grain, insects and small fish.

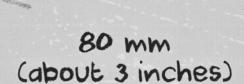

80 mm
(about 3 inches)

Geese are well-known for pooing a lot. They are less likely to do so when flying than when they are grazing. The banks of lakes are often littered with their droppings, which are thick, coiled green-brown sausages containing white uric acid and digested grass.

Western Spotted Skunk

SPILOGALE GRACILIS

The western spotted skunk is one of the skunk species of North America. It feeds on eggs, small mammals, grasshoppers and scorpions. Skunks are well known for spraying smelly liquid from their bottoms but this is nothing to do with poo. It is a special chemical to scare off predators.

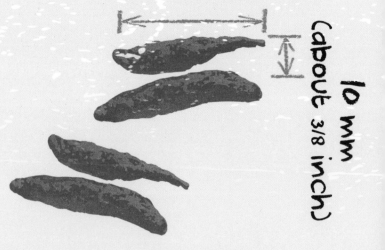

30–50 mm (about 1 5/8 inches)

10 mm (about 3/8 inch)

Skunk droppings look similar to those of a cat and have blunt ends. They often contain bits of undigested insects, berry seeds, fur or feathers. Fresh scat is black and moist, while older skunk droppings are faded and crumbly.

American Mink NEOVISON VISON

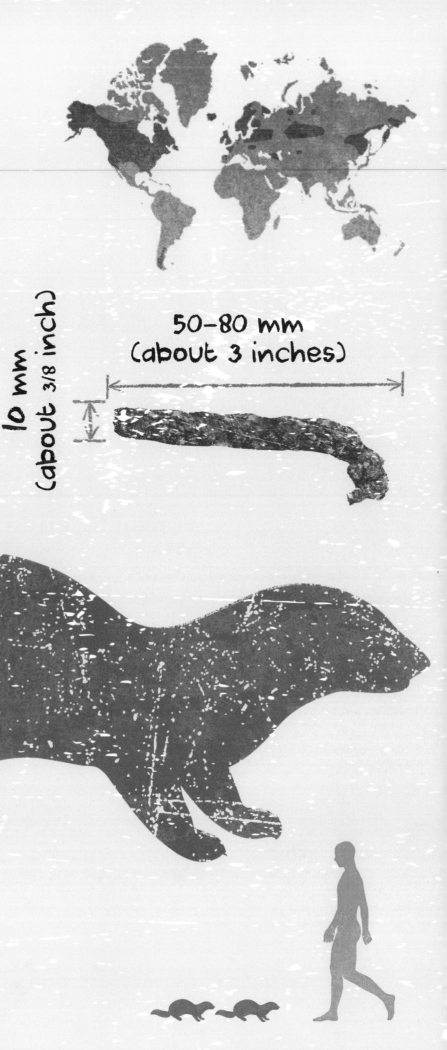

A mink can look similar to an otter, but it is smaller, has darker fur and a smaller face. It is a fierce hunter and is known to kill other animals even when it is not hungry. Its usual prey are waterfowl, birds, fish and small mammals such as water voles. Mink live near rivers and lakes, where they catch their prey.

10 mm (about 3/8 inch)

50–80 mm (about 3 inches)

American mink droppings or spraints are often found by fallen trees, weirs and bridges. Mink spraints are greenish-black and usually contain fur, fish scales and bone. Unlike otters' spraint, minks' have a foul fishy smell.

European Hedgehog

ERINACEUS EUROPAEUS

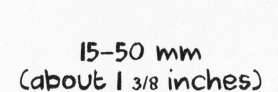

Hedgehogs are well-known for being able to roll themselves into a ball of spines if under threat. These spines (about 7,000 of them) can be raised with powerful muscles along their back.

15–50 mm
(about 1 3/8 inches)

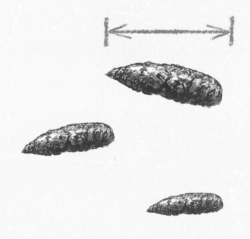

Hedgehog poo is sausage-like in shape. It is usually shiny and squidgy, and may be tapered at one end.

Normally black in colour, hedgehog droppings may contain berry pips and will often 'glisten' due to being packed with the remains of insects, such as shimmering beetle wings.

Hedgehogs can travel for a mile or so each night to find food such as beetles, caterpillars, earthworms, snails, slugs and berries.

Common Porcupine

ERETHIZON DORSATUM

The common porcupine is a prickly rodent, known as the North American porcupine. Apart from its furry stomach, its body is covered in up to 30,000 sharp quills. If anyone tries to attack, it rolls into a ball and sticks out all those quills. Predators such as coyotes, cougars, foxes, bears and wolves have ended up with painful quills stuck in their mouths.

15–25 mm
(about 3/4 inch)

Porcupines eat leaves, twigs, green plants and bark. They often climb trees to find food, usually at night.

Wood fibres make up a lot of porcupine scat, which may be in piles of pellets the size of macaroni at the base of trees or in a chain of droppings.

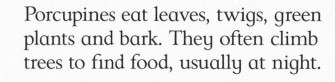

Pine Marten

MARTES MARTES

T he pine marten is a cat-sized member of the weasel family. It has dark brown fur, with a creamy-white patch at the throat. It lives in woodland, climbs trees and feeds on small rodents, birds, eggs, insects and fruit.

40-120 mm
(about 2 1/4 inches)

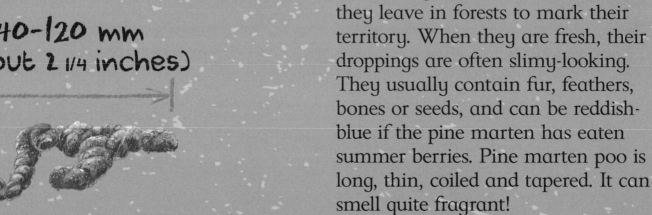

As pine martens are nocturnal and very hard to spot, you are more likely to see their scat, which they leave in forests to mark their territory. When they are fresh, their droppings are often slimy-looking. They usually contain fur, feathers, bones or seeds, and can be reddish-blue if the pine marten has eaten summer berries. Pine marten poo is long, thin, coiled and tapered. It can smell quite fragrant!

North American Raccoon

PROCYON LOTOR

Raccoons are well-known for the black fur around their eyes, as well as for their bushy tails with four to ten black rings. Raccoons have good night vision - just right for tracking down insects, worms, small animals, fish and birds' eggs, fruits, acorns and walnuts. They are good swimmers and climbers, able to withstand a drop of 12 metres (40 feet) from a tree.

Raccoon droppings are usually found under trees. A close look will show that the sides are bumpy with seeds and the tips are often rounded or broken off. A sure sign it is raccoon scat will be the remains of berries inside.

25 mm (about 1 inch)

40-70 mm (about 2 1/8 inches)

Quoll DASYURUS

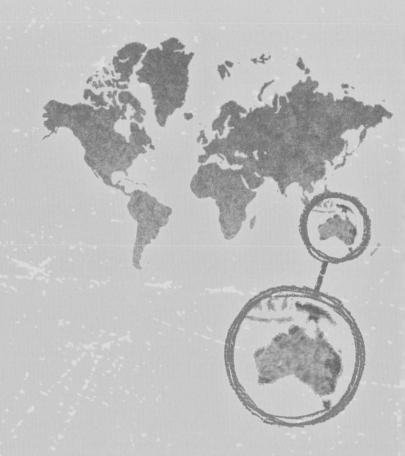

The quoll is a marsupial (a mammal that carries its young in a pouch) found in parts of Australia, Papua New Guinea and Tasmania. It looks quite similar to a domestic cat. Its scat looks quite similar to a cat's, too.

Quolls hunt at night for small mammals, birds, reptiles and insects. They also eat nuts, grasses and fruit.

83 mm (about 3 inches)

13 mm (about 3/8 inch)

Some species of quoll live alone, but visit sites where other quolls go to poo. Leaving a deposit behind is their way of saying 'Hi, it's me'.

Wombat
VOMBATIDAE

Three species of wombat live in Australia. These sturdy marsupials are the largest burrowing animals in the world. They live underground in long tunnel-and-chamber burrows which they dig with their powerful claws. They emerge from these burrows to eat grasses, roots, plants and bark - and to mark their territory with their distinctly square poo. Of all the animal poo in the world, only wombat poo is shaped like cubes.

40 mm
(about 1 5/8 inches)

25 mm
(about 1 inch)

Wombats deposit their droppings on top of rocks or logs in exposed places to announce their presence to the world. Cube-shaped droppings stack better than rounder pellets and don't roll away as easily. Just right as a unique calling card!

Royal Python

PYTHON REGIUS

T his snake, also known as a ball python, is the smallest of the African pythons and is popular as a pet. If it feels threatened it will curl into a ball rather than attack. In the wild, this 'constrictor' catches, squeezes and swallows its prey whole, such as small mammals and birds.

40–50 mm (about 1 3/4 inches)

20 mm (about 3/4 inch)

Snakes don't tend to eat and poo regularly, but when the droppings emerge, they tend to be in sloppy, dark brown, tapered chunks. As their poo dries, it turns chalkier.

Just before shedding its skin, a python may produce a much larger poo from a slit near the base of its tail.

Red Fox
VULPES VULPES

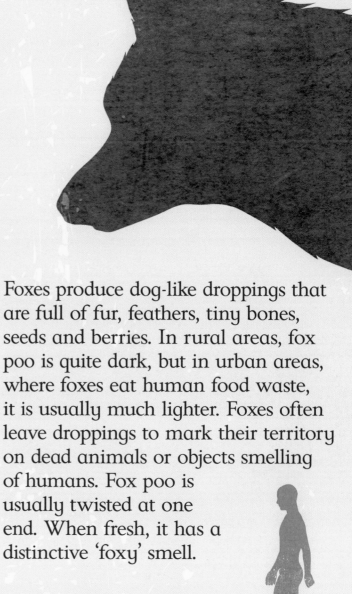

The red fox is well-known for being clever at finding food. Just ask any chicken farmer. Foxes eat lots of things, from fruits, berries and grasses to birds, squirrels, rabbits and mice. They also eat plenty of crickets, caterpillars, grasshoppers and beetles, often storing food under leaves or snow to eat later.

50-200 mm
(about 4 1/4 inches)

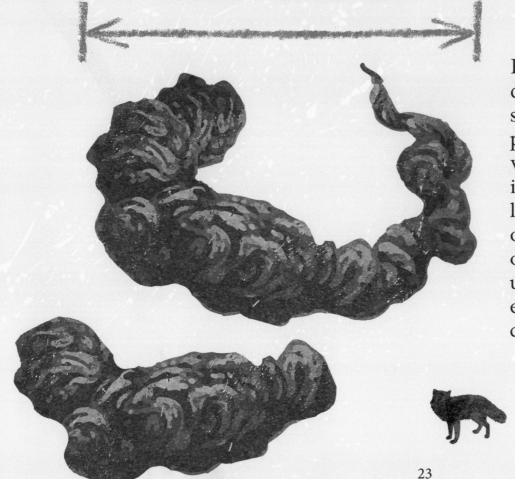

Foxes produce dog-like droppings that are full of fur, feathers, tiny bones, seeds and berries. In rural areas, fox poo is quite dark, but in urban areas, where foxes eat human food waste, it is usually much lighter. Foxes often leave droppings to mark their territory on dead animals or objects smelling of humans. Fox poo is usually twisted at one end. When fresh, it has a distinctive 'foxy' smell.

Wild Boar SUS SCROFA

Wild boar have grey-brown hair, with stocky powerful bodies. Adult male boar have tusks. They can become aggressive if threatened. Boar have poor eyesight, but a strong sense of smell.

80-100 mm (about 3 1/2 inches)

Boar use their nose to find food and detect danger. Boar are not fussy eaters and forage a wide variety of food. They eat most plants, roots, seeds and fruit, but they will also eat grubs, small mammals, birds' eggs and chicks if they find them.

Wild boar droppings are sausage shaped and lumpy. They are black when fresh, but turn grey before breaking into separate fragments.

Giant Panda AILUROPODA

Giant pandas are tree-climbing bears that live in bamboo forests in the mountains of China. These shy animals prefer to live alone much of the time, spending about 14 hours a day just eating bamboo.

76 mm (about 3 inches)

152 mm (about 5 inches)

Panda cubs eat their parents' green olive-shaped droppings, because they contain nutrients and important microbes. Scientists study giant panda scat in the wild to discover how this vulnerable species survives.

Bamboo isn't an easy food for them to digest so they have to eat a lot of it. Eating all that fibre each day (over 10 kg or 22 lb of green shoots) means that they poo up to 40 times a day.

Coyote
CANIS LATRANS

Although smaller than a wolf, the coyote is also known as the prairie wolf. It is found from Central America to as far north as Alaska. The name 'coyote' is from the Mexican for 'barking dog'. Coyotes dig burrows to shelter inside or take over burrows made by badgers.

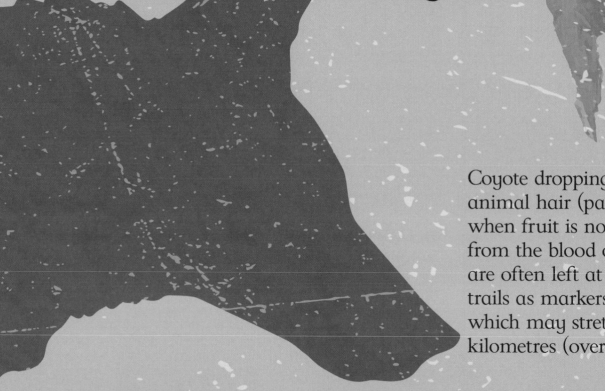

100 mm
(about 4 inches)

20 mm
(about 3/4 inch)

Coyote droppings tend to be full of animal hair (particularly in the winter when fruit is not available) and dark from the blood of their prey. Droppings are often left at cross roads and along trails as markers of a coyote's territory, which may stretch to almost 20 kilometres (over 12 miles).

Coyotes hunt prey such as squirrels, snakes, birds, lizards, deer, mice and livestock. They will also eat fruit, plants and insects.

Grey Wolf
CANIS LUPUS

Also known as the timber wolf, a grey wolf can be brown, black or white. Packs of grey wolves normally hunt together and are able to catch large prey such as moose or deer. Lone wolves will kill sheep, goats and other farm animals, or rabbits and squirrels. With such a heavy meat diet, a wolf's droppings will usually be larger and chunkier than a coyote's.

Wolf scat is often large, ropey and tapered on one or both ends. It contains fur, bones, hide and meat. Scat made of all meat and internal organs can be in various shapes. Like coyotes, wolves use their scat to mark territories and communicate to fellow wolves about their presence, status, health and identity.

100-150 mm
(about 5 inches)

30 mm
(about 1 1/4 inches)

Eurasian Lynx

LYNX LYNX

The Eurasian lynx is the largest of four species of lynx. Today it is the third largest predator in Europe (after the grey wolf and the brown bear). In winter, the lynx grows a thick silvery-grey coat and hunts by stalking prey such as deer and smaller animals. It is able to survive in wild, snowy areas. Its distinctive tufted ears provide this large wild cat with excellent hearing.

Lynx scat is left in segments with blunt ends. Like many cats, a lynx will often try to cover its droppings by scratching leaf litter and soil around or over them.

20 mm
(about 3/4 inch)

100 mm
(about 4 inches)

Cougar
PUMA CONCOLOR

Also called pumas, mountain lions and panthers, cougars are the fourth largest cat species in the world (after lions, tigers and jaguars). They are powerful hunters and eat any animal they can catch, from insects to large deer or moose.

Cougar scat usually appears as a ropey, segmented cord or a cluster of chunks. The end of one of the loose segments often shows a tapered tail. Because they eat nothing but meat, cougars' scat is full of hair and fragments of bone. Depending on its age, the scat may be black, brown, or greyish white - and is likely to have a strong smell.

25 mm (about 1 inch)

130 mm (about 5 inches)

Black Bear
URSUS AMERICANUS

The American black bear is the world's most common bear species. It lives in many woodland areas of North America and tends to keep away from people, unlike the more aggressive brown bear. Even so, their strong sense of smell makes them frequent visitors to rubbish bins on campsites. In forests, they eat mostly plants, roots, small mammals, insects and lizards.

50 mm (about 2 inches)

80-110 mm (about 3 1/2 inches)

When bears feast on berries, their droppings can be very dark and full of pips and purple juice. Bear scat can be made up of seeds and berry skins, with a few wasp remains. Bears like to dig up wasp nests and eat them.

Moose

ALCES ALCES

Moose are the largest members of the deer family, with males weighing over 600 kg (94 stone). Although not normally aggressive, males with heavy antlers may charge if they feel threatened.

Moose eat many varieties of plants, which affect the shape of their droppings. When they eat woody twigs, moose leave scat like smooth, round stones. In summer, when they eat grass and leaves, their scat is much softer and looser - more like cowpats. This poo can look similar to bear scat, although it won't have any bits of undigested food or seeds inside.

Some people even collect moose pellets, coat them in varnish and wear them as jewellery. How about a moose poo pendant? Deer droppings are sometimes known as fumet.

20 mm (about 3/4 inch)

20–30 mm (about 3/4 inch)

Northern Giraffe

GIRAFFA CAMELOPARDALIS

As the world's tallest mammal, up to 6.1 metres (20 feet), the giraffe can reach high into acacia trees to eat leaves. When all those leaves have been digested, the resulting droppings fall from a great height and scatter everywhere - like a shower of olives.

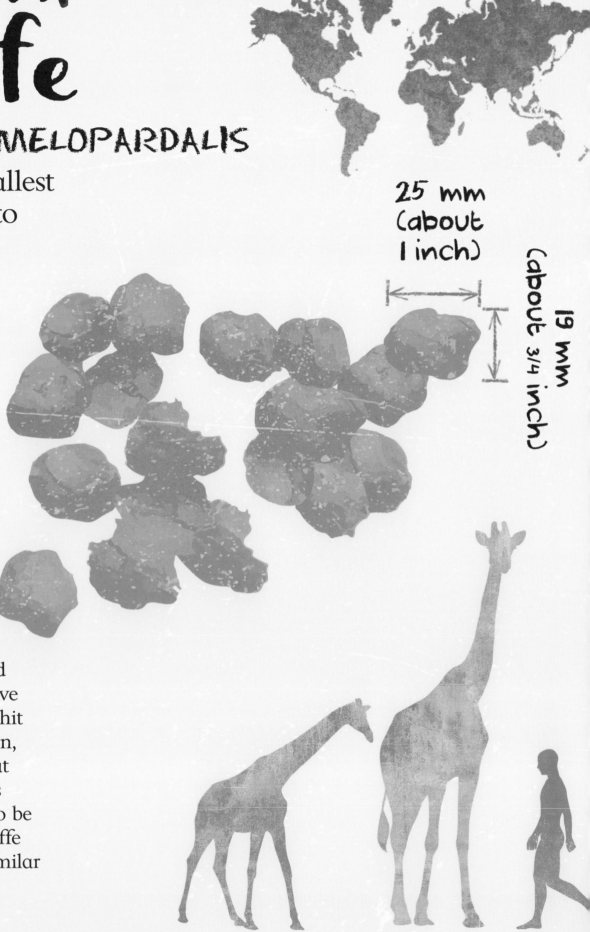

25 mm (about 1 inch)

19 mm (about 3/4 inch)

A giraffe produces small, round balls of dung which tend to have a dent on one side where they hit the ground. The colour is brown, which is typical of animals that feed off trees, rather than grass feeders where the dung tends to be blacker. Some trackers say giraffe poo is fairly sweet-smelling (similar to acacia honey!).

Mountain Gorilla

GORILLA BERINGEI BERINGEI

Mountain gorillas are now very rare, with only a few hundred left on Earth. Most live in the forests of the Virunga mountains in central Africa.

Gorillas eat roots, shoots, fruit, wild celery, tree bark, pulp and insects. A large adult male can weigh over 200 kg (441 lb) and eat over 30 kg (66 lb) of vegetation a day. Their droppings help scientists work out how many gorillas are left in these remote forests.

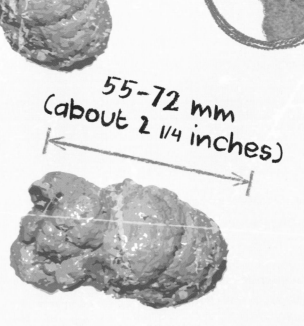

55-72 mm (about 2 1/4 inches)

At each nest site, scientists measure dung sizes to find out the ages of individual gorillas in a group. By studying these 'scat records' over time, they will learn how the numbers and health of mountain gorillas are changing.

African Lion

PANTHERA LEO

Lions are at the top of the African food chain, as they hunt large prey and eat nothing but meat. When lions hunt together, they can kill and eat large buffalo or zebra.

45 mm
(about 1 3/4 inches)

750 mm
(about 29 1/2 inches)

You might think eating zebra makes
lion dung stripy! In fact, lion poo often
has light and dark stripes, whatever
animal it eats. That's because when
they catch their prey, lions tend to gorge
on the juicy meat first. The blood makes
their poo dark. Then, lions spend hours
gnawing on their prey's bones. This
makes the next stretch of poo white.
Sometimes that means a light patch on
the end of a very long poo.

Boa Constrictor

BOA CONSTRICTOR

Boa constrictors are large snakes found in Central and South America. Pythons and anacondas belong to the same family as the boa. Boa constrictors often reach 4 metres (13 feet) or even longer.

These snakes live in deserts and rainforests - some in underground holes and others in trees. They hunt at night, eating birds and mammals. Their bite is not poisonous; they kill their prey by seizing it in their jaws, then coiling their powerful body around it. This crushes their prey to death, cutting off the blood supply. After a large meal, a boa constrictor may not need to eat again for many weeks.

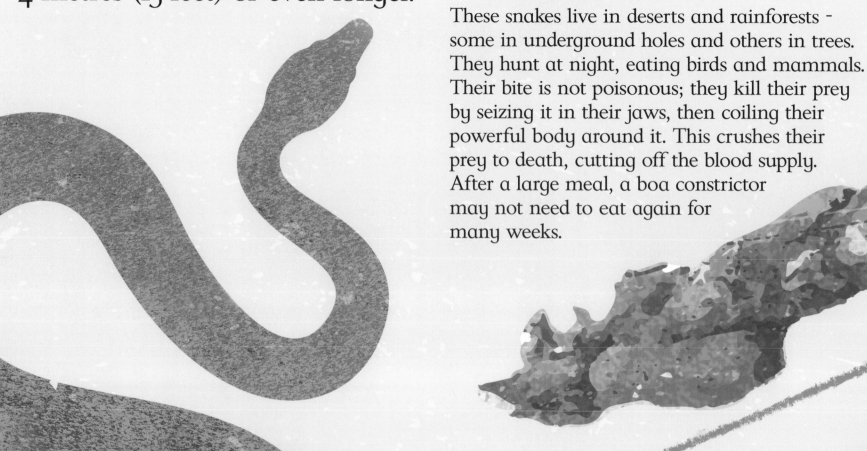

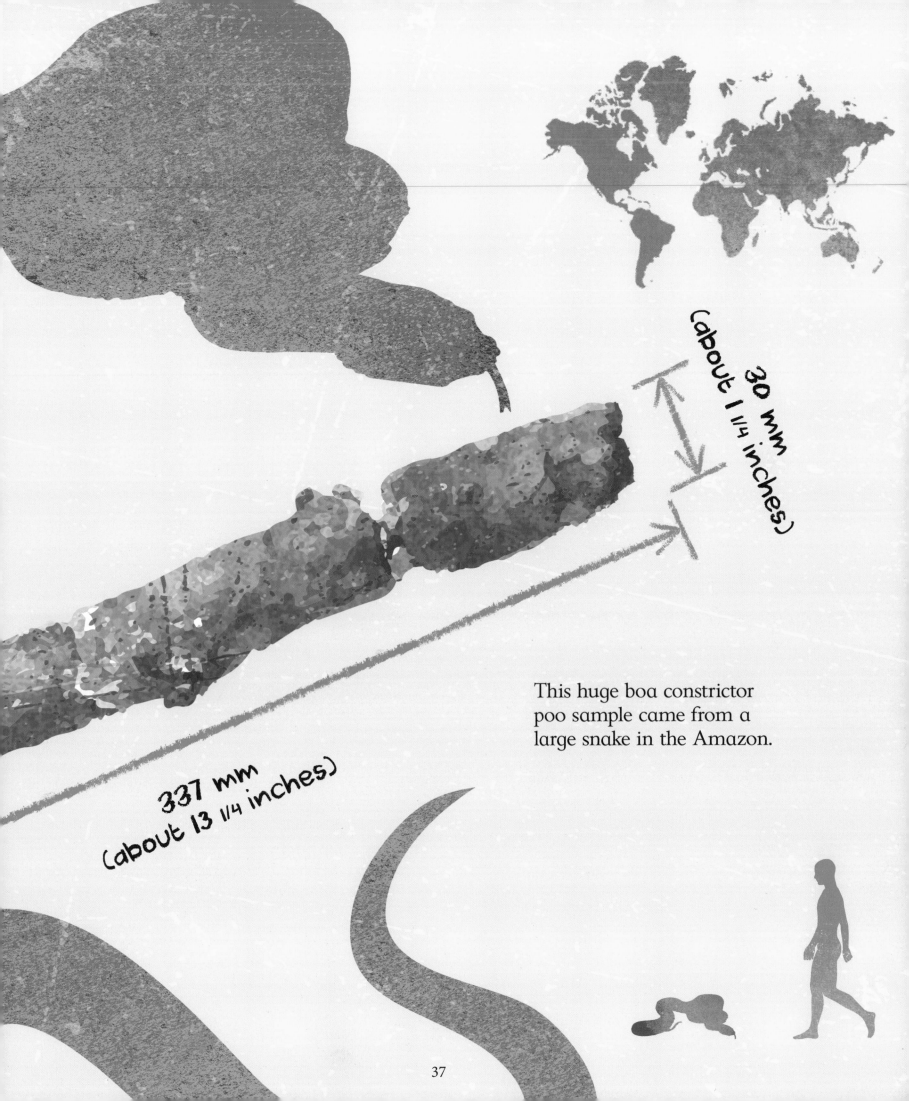

30 mm
(about 1 1/4 inches)

337 mm
(about 13 1/4 inches)

This huge boa constrictor poo sample came from a large snake in the Amazon.

Bison

BISON BISON

300 mm (about 12 inches)

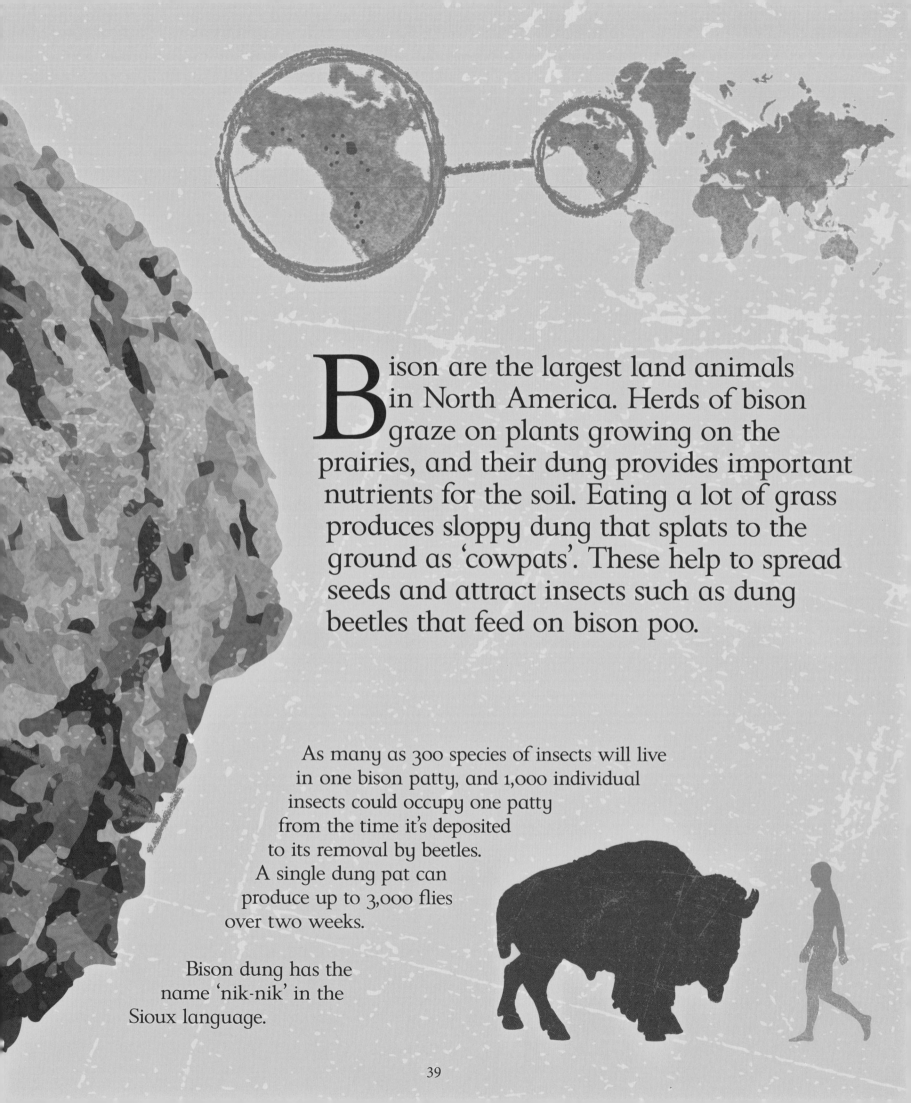

Bison are the largest land animals in North America. Herds of bison graze on plants growing on the prairies, and their dung provides important nutrients for the soil. Eating a lot of grass produces sloppy dung that splats to the ground as 'cowpats'. These help to spread seeds and attract insects such as dung beetles that feed on bison poo.

As many as 300 species of insects will live in one bison patty, and 1,000 individual insects could occupy one patty from the time it's deposited to its removal by beetles. A single dung pat can produce up to 3,000 flies over two weeks.

Bison dung has the name 'nik-nik' in the Sioux language.

White Rhinoceros

CERATOTHERIUM SIMUM

The rhinoceros has poor eyesight and depends on its sense of smell. That's important when it comes to rhino poo. Scientists have studied white rhinos' dung heaps in South Africa and found that these huge mammals leave messages for other rhinos in their huge poo piles.

Each rhino leaves different chemicals in its poo, which other rhinos can smell to get clues about what's going on with all the rhinos in the group. It's like their form of social media.

A team of UK-based scientists is collecting rhinoceros droppings to help save endangered rhinos in Africa. Called 'Saving species with faeces', the project studies poo-data to manage the health of these animals.

100 mm (about 4 inches)

EACH BALL
IN A PILE:

150 mm
(about 6 inches)

African Elephant

LOXODONTA AFRICANA

An African savannah elephant can grow to 9 metres (almost 30 feet) from trunk to tail and weigh 5,440 kilograms (over 5 tonnes). It is the largest land mammal on the planet and is now a threatened species.

Elephants only eat plants - about 50 kg (110 lb) of vegetation each day. Much of this tough, fibrous food passes through their bodies undigested. Mixed with over 200 litres (53 gallons) of water that it must drink every day, an adult African elephant can produce over 100 kg (220 lb) of dung in a day.

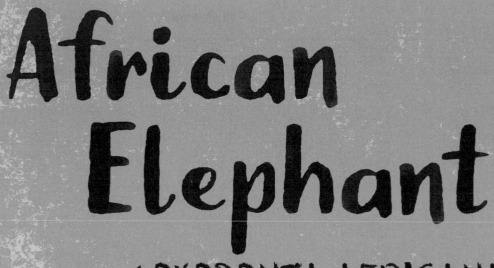

EACH BALL
IN A PILE:

150 mm
(about 6 inches)

African Elephant

LOXODONTA AFRICANA

An African savannah elephant can grow to 9 metres (almost 30 feet) from trunk to tail and weigh 5,440 kilograms (over 5 tonnes). It is the largest land mammal on the planet and is now a threatened species.

Elephants only eat plants - about 50 kg (110 lb) of vegetation each day. Much of this tough, fibrous food passes through their bodies undigested. Mixed with over 200 litres (53 gallons) of water that it must drink every day, an adult African elephant can produce over 100 kg (220 lb) of dung in a day.

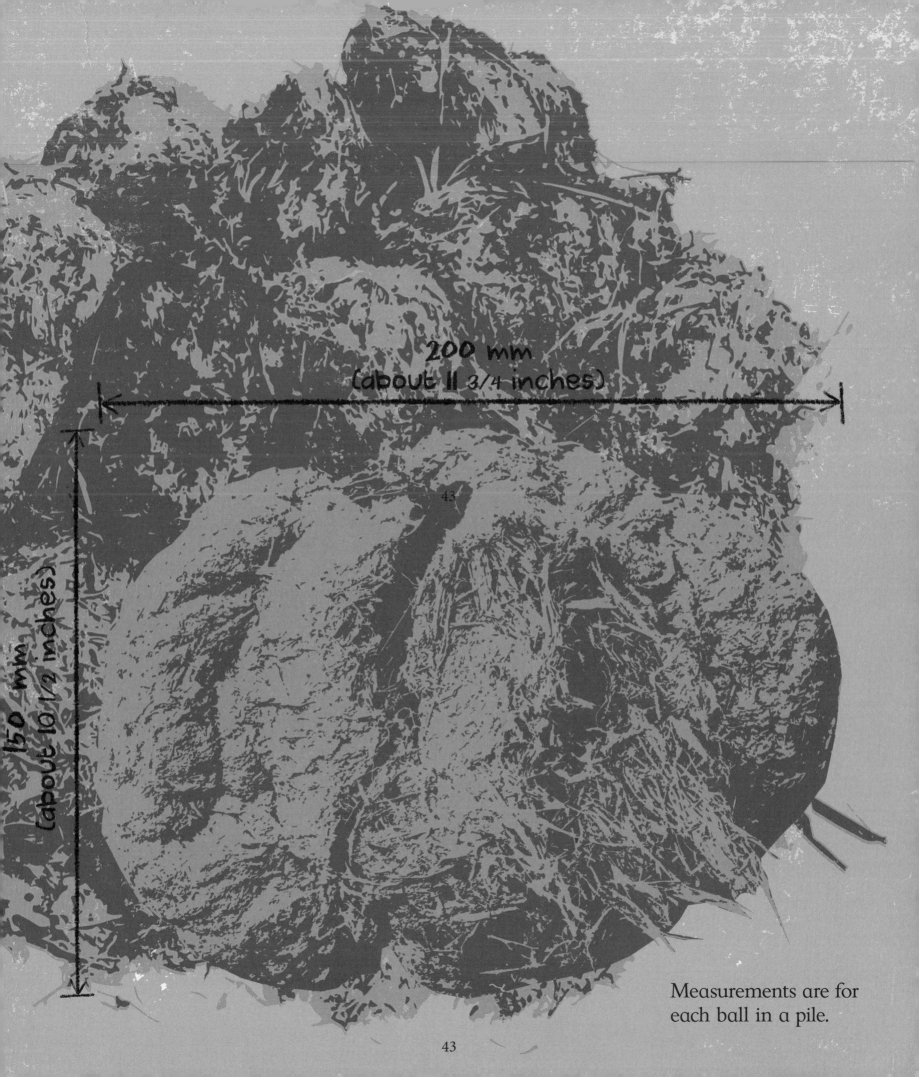

200 mm
(about 11 3/4 inches)

150 mm
(about 10 1/2 inches)

Measurements are for
each ball in a pile.

43

160 mm
(about 6 1/4 inches)

Tyrannosaurus Rex

TYRANNOSAURUS REX

The huge meat-eating dinosaur Tyrannosaurus rex lived about 65 to 70 million years ago. Its fossilised remains have been found in North America – and so has its poo. Tyrannosaurus rex coprolite is king-size and one famous specimen from Canada is packed with bone fragments. These bone fragments are what's left of dinosaurs this scary predator hunted and devoured.

440 mm (about 17 3/8 inches)

Ancient Crocodile

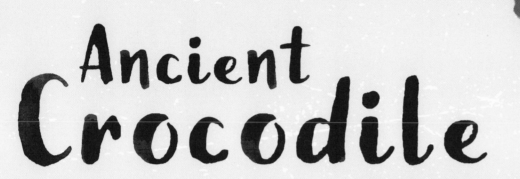

DEINOSUCHUS

Huge crocodiles once lived during the time of the dinosaurs and they left lumps of their poo behind. Experts have studied this solid, fossilised dung called coprolite from millions of years ago.

The size, shape and nature of the dung show that a large ancient crocodile called Deinosuchus ('terrible crocodile') probably ate sea turtles and dinosaurs. It hunted in what is now the United States and northern Mexico, where its poo was buried in sediment and fossilised. In 2014, one of the longest-known coprolites sold for over $10,000.

Tyrannosaurus Rex

TYRANNOSAURUS REX

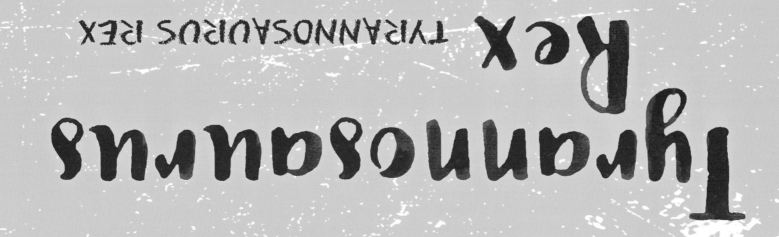

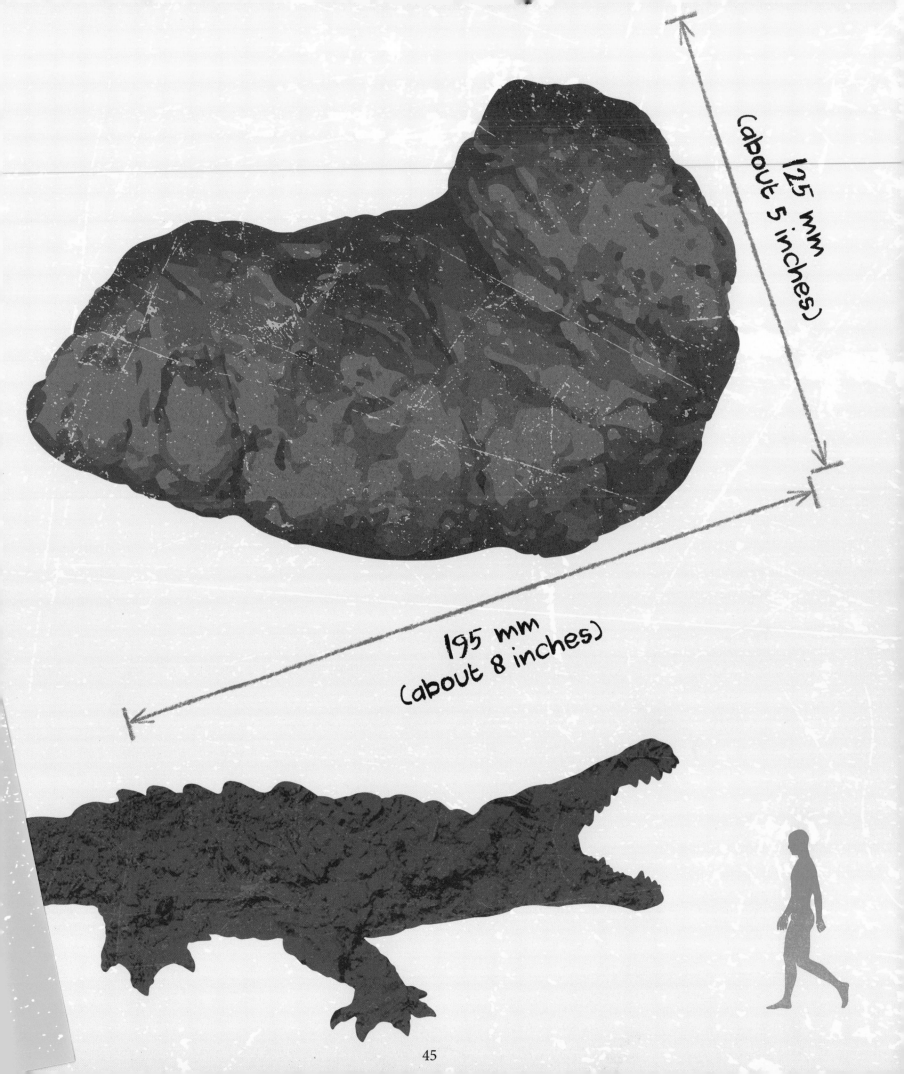

125 mm
(about 5 inches)

195 mm
(about 8 inches)

Tyrannosaurus rex was the only meat-eating dinosaur from this time and place to produce such large coprolite. There is fossil evidence that Tyrannosaurus rex crushed bones before swallowing them, as the bones in the coprolite samples are all broken into small fragments. After all, this fearsome dinosaur had the strongest ever bite of any land animal.

Glossary

Bacteria
Tiny living cells all around us that we can't see.

Coprolite
A piece of fossilised dung.

Endangered
At risk of disappearing forever.

Faeces
The correct term for poo (also called droppings, dung, excrement, scat, stools).

Guano
The faeces of seabirds or bats, often used as a fertiliser.

Mammals
Warm-blooded animals that nourish their young with milk.

Microbe
A very small living thing that can only be seen with a microscope.

Nocturnal
Active at night.

Nutrient
Important material that plants and animals need to live and grow.

Predator
An animal that hunts and eats other animals.

Prey
An animal that is killed and eaten by other animals.

Uric acid
A white substance expelled from the bodies of birds, reptiles and insects.

Index

Author:

John Townsend worked as a secondary school teacher before becoming a full time writer of children's books and a writer-in-residence in a primary school tree-house. He specialises in fun, exciting information books for reluctant readers, as well as fast-paced fiction, reading schemes and 'fiction with facts' books. He visits schools around the country to encourage excitement in all aspects of reading and writing. He has written other titles in the *Life-Sized* series so can often be found crawling with a ruler in the undergrowth.

Wildlife consultant:

The National Poo Museum is based in Sandown on the Isle of Wight. The world is covered in poo and our lives depend on it in ways most of us never imagine. The National Poo Museum exists to explore and celebrate this extraordinary stuff which is around and inside us all!

Series creator:

David Salariya was born in Dundee, Scotland. He has illustrated a wide range of books and has created and designed many new series for publishers in the UK and overseas. David established The Salariya Book Company in 1989. He lives in Brighton, England, with his wife, illustrator Shirley Willis, and their son, Jonathan.

Editor:
Nick Pierce

Acknowledgements:

With thanks to scat experts who have helped check information in this book. Scatology, the study of biological excrement, faeces and dung has provided a pile of useful answers.

Also, with thanks to Steve, the royal python in Exeter, for making a sizable contribution to this book.

Thanks to the giant pandas at Zoo Atlanta, Georgia, USA, and Adelaide Zoo, Australia for providing a drop of data for our records.

Published in Great Britain in MMXX by Book House, an imprint of **The Salariya Book Company Ltd** 25 Marlborough Place, Brighton BN1 1UB **www.salariya.com**

ISBN: 978-1-912904-57-0

1 3 5 7 9 8 6 4 2

A CIP catalogue record for this book is available from the British Library.

Printed and bound in China.

Visit
www.salariya.com
for our online catalogue and
free fun stuff.

PAPER FROM
SUSTAINABLE
FORESTS